MW00931758

you
deserve
to be
happy

billie brooks

you deserve to be happy

Copyright © 2024 Billie Brooks

All rights reserved. No portion of this book may be reproduced in any form without permission from the publisher, except as permitted by U.S. copyright law. For permissions contact:
billiebrookspoetry@gmail.com

ISBN: 9798876701954

chapters

chapter 1:

the end

the hardest thing in life
is finally finding the person
you can't live without
and then having to live
without them

you deserve to be happy

you told me
you were afraid to lose me
until you decided
to face your fear
and left

and just like that
we are back to being
strangers

i know
people come and go
but you said
you will never leave

i don't hate you
i just hate that i keep hoping
we will find our way back
to each other again

i don't hate you
i just hate that my heart
keeps breaking
because of you

i don't hate you
i just hate the fact that
you are not hurting
as much as i am

i don't hate you
but i think
i am starting to

one day
you will look back
at what we had
and regret everything
you did
to destroy it

have you ever
been in so much pain
that it physically
hurts inside?

the worst feeling
is when your whole life
starts falling apart
and all you can do
is to watch
helplessly

i don't know which hurts more

letting go of someone you love
or
holding on to someone
who doesn't love you back

we break
our own hearts
because we expected
too much

how do you say
goodbye
when your heart
doesn't want
to let go?

i cared too much
in a world that
cares too little

i don't know
how to let you go
without feeling like
i am losing a part of
myself

you feel the hurt
coming
but there is nothing
you can do
than let it come

some people say
it's painful to
wait for someone

some people say
it's painful to
forget someone

but the real pain comes
when you don't know
if you should wait for them
or try to forget about them

stop waiting for
something that isn't
going to happen

it's hard
to turn the page
when i know
you won't be
in the next chapter
anymore

i don't want to
give up on you
but i know
i have to

sometimes
you just have to
let go

you tried your best
and there is nothing more
you can do

stop making yourself
miserable
stop forcing things
to work out
when they are not supposed to

sometimes
things just don't work out
and that's okay

let go
of the things
that have let go
of you

stop chasing someone
who is okay with
losing you

it is not love
if you are the only one
fighting for it

someone
giving you less
doesn't mean
you have to try harder

no reason to stay
is a good reason
to leave

not every relationship
is supposed to be
beautiful
and long-lasting

some people
come into your life
to show you
what's right and what's wrong

some people
come into your life
to show you
who you can be

some people
come into your life
to teach you
how to love yourself

learn the lessons
enjoy the moments
but when the time comes,
let them go

stop holding on
to someone
just because you
have a history together

you have to let go
of the thing
that's breaking you
even if it breaks you
to let go

never let someone
mistreat you
just because
you love them

stop wondering
if they still
care about you

if you have to ask
the answer is
no

you cannot
change things
by loving them
harder

i think it's time to let go
i can't keep overthinking
every scenario in my head
and blaming myself for
every mistake you made

i think it's time to let go
i tried everything i could
to be the perfect person for you
but no matter how hard i try
i was never enough

i think it's time to let go
i am losing my mind
trying to keep our memories alive
and you don't seem to
care at all

i think it's time to let go
i deserve so much
better than this
i deserve so much
better than you

it's time
to end your part
in my story

chapter 2:

a new beginning

you don't need to
have all the answers
right now

this is just a chapter
not your whole story

it's okay if everything seems to be hurting and all you feel is anxious and overwhelmed. it's okay if you are spiraling out of control and you can't stop. it's okay if you feel hopeless about everything and can't find the strength to keep going. it's okay to feel all these things. it's okay. but you need to remember this—all these feelings you are feeling right now are temporary and they will leave. and when they leave, they will leave you a much stronger person than before. so let yourself feel whatever you are feeling and do whatever you need to do to heal. it's okay if it's taking a long time. it's okay if none of it makes sense right now. you will get there.

let it hurt
until it doesn't
hurt anymore
then let it go

you are not
going to
feel like this
forever

you have survived
everything so far
you are going to
survive this too

someone once told me

the person who overthinks
is also the person who
overfeels

and i really felt that

stop losing yourself
trying to hold onto someone
who doesn't care about
losing you

if you feel like you can't make it through the day, focus on the next hour. if you feel like you can't make it through the next hour, focus on the next few minutes. if you feel like you can't make it through the next few minutes, take it one breath at a time.

- *an advice that saved me*

you deserve to be happy

i hope the pain
eases soon

sometimes
you think that
you want to disappear
but all you really want
is to be found

this pain will only
make you stronger

it's normal to
still miss the person
who hurt you

but that doesn't
change the fact that
you have to let them go

i hope you will
never see yourself
as a failure
just because
you weren't the person
they wanted

you don't have to put on a brave face and be strong every day. it's okay to drop that armor and let yourself crumble when you don't feel fine. if you can't get out of bed, take a rest day and sleep in. if you don't have the capacity to do anything, get under a blanket and put on a movie. and if you feel the need to scream and cry, do it with all your heart. the sky does it all the time and it still shines the next day.

- *it's okay to be sad*

you deserve to be happy

this
feeling
will
pass

stop saying
it's okay
when it's not

you deserve to be
someone's first choice,
not their backup option

you deserve to be
loved and cherished,
not taken for granted

you can't heal
if you keep trying to
go back to the thing
that broke you

sometimes
the person you want
the most
is the person
you are best without

things fall apart
so better things can
fall together

someday
you will see that
letting go and moving on
is the best decision
you could have made

it might be hard
to believe
but you won't
feel this way forever

someday soon
this pain
you are feeling
won't be so unbearable

but for now
take a deep breath
and let yourself feel
everything you are feeling

treat yourself kindly
and remember
these feelings won't
last forever

you can't hate yourself
into a better version

- *be kind*

things not working out
right now
doesn't mean
life is going terribly

it just means that
it's not meant to be
at this time
and that's okay

put on relaxing music
draw a bath
cleanse your body
wash away the negative thoughts
drink some water
get into bed
breathe

no matter
how hard you try
things won't always go
the way you want them to

you might lose
the person
you thought was
the love of your life

you might lose
the friends
you thought will
always be there for you

you might lose
pieces of yourself
you never imagined
will be gone

but before you realize it
new love enters
better friends come along
and a stronger and wiser you
is staring back at the mirror

dear me,

i know you are scared
but you got this

you don't always
need to try your best

sometimes
you just need to
breathe and
let it go

it's time
to start loving yourself
instead of loving the idea
of other people
loving you

take a deep breath
and remember

when you let go
you are making space
for better things to
come into your life

this is just the beginning
of your story
it is going to get better
from here

chapter 3:

one day at a time

it's okay
if it's taking more time
than you thought
to get through all of this

give yourself
the permission
to not always have
your shit together

you don't have to feel hopeful about the future.
it's enough to just be curious about what is
coming.

- *an advice my therapist gave me*

today
focus more on
what you can do
and less on
what you can't do

you deserve to be happy

i know it feels heavy
right now
but it will pass
and you
will be happy again

you deserve to be happy

you will get through this
just like you always do

sometimes
what didn't work out for you
really worked out for you

you will never need
to force something
that is meant for you

you don't always
need to have a plan

sometimes
you just need to breathe
and believe that
better things are coming

you still have time
to achieve the things
you want

forgive yourself
for all the mistakes
you have made
when you didn't know better

you can start over
as many times
as you need to

i think it's brave that
you get up every morning
even on the days where
your soul ache for a rest

i think it's brave that
you keep holding on
even on the days where
you don't see a reason to

i think it's brave that
you push through every obstacles
even on the days where
you are tired of trying

i think it's brave that
even on the days where
you feel like giving up
you never do

you have whatever it takes
to get through this

it's okay
if you are
still healing
from the things
you don't talk about

that little progress
you have made today
matters

this is a reminder to slow down and be gentle with yourself. you have been through a lot the last few weeks and you need to give yourself some time to breathe and reset. take as long as you need.

- *you deserve it*

you are not too much.
you are not too sensitive.
you are not too needy.
you are not too emotional.
you are not too quiet.
you are not too anything.

you don't deserve
any less
just because
you were not
at your best today

you are whole
worthy
loved
even when all you did
was try to survive

i'm slowly learning
how to miss someone
without
wanting them back

sometimes
you have to walk away
from everything you wanted
to find everything
you never knew you needed

just because
it's taking awhile
doesn't mean
it's not happening

life is a journey
not a race
keep going
at your own pace

give yourself some credit
for the days
you made it through
when you thought
you couldn't

you didn't go through
all of that for nothing

to the person i am today:

i promise i will start taking care of you again.
i promise i will start being kind to you again.
i promise i will start listening to your needs again.
i promise i will start loving you again.

i see the progress you are making
and i'm so proud of you

keep taking
these baby steps

it might not feel like
you are moving forward

but one day
you will look back
and realize how far
you have come

you deserve to be happy

step by step
day by day

- *you got this*

you haven't even met
the best version of
yourself

- *don't give up*

someday
you will look back
and see that not giving up
is the best decision
you have ever made

chapter 4:

you deserve to be happy

you can't go back
and change
the beginning of your story
but you can start
where you are
and change the ending

the pain
might have hurt you
but it did not
destroy you

don't fall back
into your old patterns
just because
they are familiar

you deserve a life
filled with happiness
and positivity

stop giving
so much of yourself
to people who will not
do the same

you can be
a nice person
and still
say no

no more settling for bare minimums.
no more negative self-talks.
no more people pleasing.
no more trying to force things.
no more lowering standards.

you deserve so much more than that.

i am going to make a
beautiful life for myself
no matter what it takes

- *a promise to myself*

stop trying to
be liked by people
you don't even like

don't you ever allow
your loneliness
to lower your standards

you deserve to be
with someone
you can message
even the smallest parts
of your day to

you deserve to be
with someone
who is interested in
whatever you have to say
even if it's the most
random thing in the world

you deserve to be
with someone
who knows everything about you
from how you like your coffee
to what keeps you awake at night

you deserve to be
with someone
who makes you feel loved
and valued

you deserve
a love that stays
even when it's hard to

especially when
it's hard to

don't you ever
shrink yourself
to make other people
feel comfortable

if it makes you happy
it doesn't have to
make sense
to others

stop giving
your energy to people
who don't deserve it

choose the people
who make you happy
and let go of the people
who don't

you don't have to
rebuild a bond
you didn't break

don't you ever apologize
for choosing yourself

fill yourself with so much
love and gratitude that
the negative things
won't have space
to come in

i hope
something good
happens to you
today

to the person i end up with:

i can't wait for the days where i get to share my life with you. the days where we go on random adventures with no destination, the days where we cuddle on the couch watching the rain fall outside our window, the days where we mess up our dinner while trying a new recipe, but we eat it anyway. the days we stay up too late because being in reality is better than being in our dreams, the days that just flash past us but we never worry about being unproductive, because we are happy. i know i haven't met you yet, but there are just so many things i can't wait to share with you. the best thing i know now is to keep working on myself, and i know one day my life will be beautiful, just the way i want it.

maybe the home
you have been looking for
is nothing
but two arms
holding you tight
when you are at your worst

you don't need to be perfect
you don't need to be the best
you just need to be yourself

you deserve to be happy

you
are
more
than
enough

the past version of you
is so proud of
how far you've come

- *keep going*

the things
you have been
praying for
are coming

to the person i was when i was at my lowest:

thank you for not giving up

you look happier
ever since
you let people lose you
instead of begging them
to choose you

despite all the pain
you have been through
you are still here
standing tall and smiling

- *there is nothing more beautiful than that*

i'm proud of you for not giving up on yourself.
i'm proud of you for making it this far.
i'm proud of you for staying strong.
i'm proud of you.

you are so
breathtakingly
beautiful

i'm so glad
you made it
through

you deserve to be happy

you deserve to be happy

Made in the USA
Las Vegas, NV
05 July 2024

91739249R00079